BRENDA WILSON

Living with Leo

The Rewards of Adopting an Adult Dog Instead of a Puppy

Contents

Dedication

Leo and I want to dedicate this effort to Aunt Ruth, Jake, and Charlie, who all passed away during the writing of this work. Aunt Ruth was 103 years old and told us beautiful stories from her long life and the things she saw over the years. Jake and Charlie were senior canines with chronic health issues but soldiered on until the end. Both passed on after short illnesses.

Leo still looks for them when we pass their houses on our walks.

1

Introduction

I didn't need a dog. I wasn't even sure I WANTED a dog. My permanent home is in Ohio, but I found myself living 1100 miles from home, caring for an elderly relative, and I REALLY didn't need a dog. But I was lonely and becoming depressed. COVID lock-downs and family health issues were beginning to take their toll. My husband remained in Ohio to tend to our home and care for our aging dog, who doesn't travel well. The evenings were long, and the house eerily quiet at times. I started to yearn for the companionship I had always enjoyed with my pets. Many people shop for designer dogs, but my family has almost always obtained our canine family members through re-homing situations.

I came to Florida to visit my mother and recover from surgery in 2018. I was appalled at the condition of my mother's health. I knew she had been having breathing issues after a severe bout of pneumonia several months before. Mom and her 99-year-old aunt, who still lived in her own home, had been watching over each other for many years. Both were widowed, and they lived right around the corner from each other.

It soon became evident that Mom required more assistance than Aunt Ruth could provide. I realized I needed to retire from my nursing job to stay in Florida to help her. I had hoped that mom might regain her strength with someone to cook for her, handle daily chores, and make sure she got to her appointments. That didn't happen. Despite a stint in a rehab facility after a fractured hip, she continued to decline and was soon using oxygen all the time.

My brother's health was also declining. He passed away from a wound infection and complications of pneumonia with COVID that he acquired while in a rehab facility.

After Mom passed away, I stayed to help Aunt Ruth. While her physical condition was amazing for 99 years old, she had reached a stage where she could not be entirely on her own. I think losing Mom and John, so close together, one and two generations younger than she was, took a mental toll. Add to that the COVID lockdown that isolated her from all her outside friends and activities; she started on a steep decline that never entirely abated, even when restrictions were lifted. The mask mandate made things even worse. With her hearing so bad, she relied on facial expressions and watching a person's mouth. She may have never HAD COVID but it never the less contributed to her death.

No, I didn't NEED a dog but having grown up with them as part of the family, I was beginning to feel the lack of that unconditional love, comfort, and companionship, especially with the depression of loss.

2

Puppy vs Adult Dog

I knew I didn't want to get a young puppy. Been there, done that, and didn't want to go there again. Yes, they are cute and cuddly with those big eyes and round faces, but they are a LOT of work. I can't count the number of shoes, flip-flops, towels, and socks our last puppy chewed up before she outgrew that stage. She almost lost her happy home when she chewed on the collar of my husband's work boots. He was NOT amused, but he did eventually forgive her.

I thought about maybe taking in a pet whose owner had passed away, a common occurrence in a 55+ community, and started watching the community bulletin board and local online sites that I located. I also checked the local pounds, the Humane Society, rescue groups, and bulletin boards. This went on for several months before I ran across a rehoming site online that allowed owners to list their own pets rather than surrender them to a rescue site.

3

The Search Begins

I knew I wanted a small breed dog or mix, one that could easily go along with us when we traveled, a retirement goal of my husband and mine. By putting that in the search criteria along with the location (and how far I was willing to travel), I got some interesting results from Yorkies to Beagles (I had never considered Beagles as "small dogs" before.)

I eventually sent email requests for information about two, a Yorkie and a Pekingese, and was ready to set a date to meet the Yorkie named Bella when her owner changed her mind about re-homing. Her kids had a fit when they discovered they might be losing her. Though disappointed, I could understand. If you view your pet as a family member, the thought of losing one is gut-wrenching. The search went on.

4

Discovering Leo

I ran across a cute little dog on a re-homing site called "Get Your Pet.". He was located about 50 miles away. I filled out the form and eventually received a reply from the owner. After some back-and-forth text messaging, we arranged to meet at a park near her home on Labor Day.

I drove to Tampa, about an hour away, and something I would have hated to do on a typical work day due to traffic. Thank goodness the majority of traffic on this Holiday weekend was headed west/east, to and from the beaches, not north to Tampa. I made it in good time, and using Google Maps, I located the park without much trouble. When we met up, I was enchanted with the friendly bundle of fur that was Leo. His shiny black eyes were intensely intelligent, and he was very serene in the significantly large crowd of people at the park. He even maintained his calm when a toddler ran up and wanted to pet him.

Leo was a 2-year-old Shih Tzu/Bichon Frise mix and looked to have inherited the best of both breeds. He was very well-behaved and quiet, a significant plus to find in a small breed dog. Even though he came from a breeder, I don't feel I compromised my commitment to not support breeding for profit since I did not buy him from the breeder, I was hoping to "rescue" him.

We sat and talked for quite a while. The owners were a student couple from Qatar, attending Tampa University. They were in their final semester of school and preparing to return to their home. Qatar, as an Arab country, with the predominant religion's cultural dislike of dogs as pets, made them reluctant to try to take Leo back with them. The expense and logistics of transporting him such a long way were also concerns. She was very attached to him and wanted to make sure he went to a home where he would be loved and treated well.

She explained that I was one of five applicants that she was meeting over a couple of days before deciding on who to place him with. I happened to be the last on her list to interview. The only contender worked full time and would have to keep him locked in a kennel, in her apartment, for about 10 hours a day. That was a situation she wanted to avoid, if possible. We talked for about an hour and a half about Leo and my prior pets and what my daily life was like. The fact that I was retired and would be at home or able to take him with me most of the time was the deciding factor for her.

I had assumed that I would have to wait for her decision and maybe drive back to Tampa to pick him up at a later date if I was her choice. It shocked me when she offered to let me take him right then, with all his belongings! We walked back to her apartment (virtually across the street), and she and her husband helped me get his kennel, bedding toys, and nearly a month's worth of food to my car. She emailed me copies of all his records since she got him as a puppy

I was very happy. Thank goodness Leo is a good traveler. He curled up in the passenger seat and slept most of the way home.

5

Life With Leo

Leo was quiet at first. He followed me from room to room and just watched. We walked up and down the street and around the house that evening to acquaint him with his new neighborhood. I showed him where I put his food and water, but he wasn't hungry. I fixed him a bed in my room that night, but within minutes he was up on the bed, cuddled in behind my knees. He made it abundantly clear that it was where he intended to sleep and HAS slept every night since.

We fell into a routine that suited us both in short order. I confined him in his kennel the first few times I had to leave him alone for any length of time, but that didn't last long. Next, I closed him in the sunroom with the TV on. He could sleep on the couch and chew on a treat. He was quite comfortable with his food and water dishes, toys, and a potty pad. He behaved so well that he now has the run of the house when I'm gone. He sleeps on a recliner or the couch until he hears the car in the drive.

He charmed my morning walking companions with his captivating personality. Their dogs checked him over thoroughly and decided he was acceptable for their group. He gets along with all the other animals we encounter on our walks, including cats.....at least so far.

Our days usually start with him deciding that I need to get up about 10 minutes before the alarm. We don't actually need an alarm, but it encourages me to get out of bed and ready myself to meet our friends for our walk (I still snooze the alarm for as long as he'll let me). He lays across my shoulders and tries to lick my ears and face to ensure I'm awake. That usually prods me enough to roll out of bed. He generally waits patiently (carefully observing my every move to head off any thought of crawling back into bed. I am NOT a morning person). I go through my morning routine and get dressed, but as soon as I head toward the bedroom door, he is right on my heels.....literally. He steps on the back of my slippers. He practically vibrates with excitement while I put on my shoes and get him into his harness and leash. In the beginning, we ended our walk with our first check on Aunt Ruth before heading home. Most morning outings are anywhere from 30-60 minutes, depending mainly on the weather, and we loop several blocks. It is generally too hot for his paws on the asphalt for mid-day and later walks, so we only walk in the grass around the house and the strip of open lawn beside us. It is a favorite pit stop for all the dog walkers in the community to visit, giving Leo many interesting smells to investigate.

6

Leo and Friends

Our community, up until recently, only permitted dogs up to 25 pounds. Leo's walking buddies were a 12-year-old West Highland Terrier named Jake, a 3-year-old Chihuahua/Wippit mix named Turk (actually Turkey), and a Papillion named Charlie, who was at least as old, if not older than Jake. Charlie and Jake were arthritic and walked very slowly. Charlie was toothless but still wanted to bite if he thought someone was getting too grabby. Turk, on the other hand, is a young maniac. He may weigh all of 10 pounds, but he has the attitude of a Doberman junkyard dog. He growls, barks, and lunges at just about everything; birds, other dogs or cats, bunnies, geckos, strangers, golf carts, bicycles, or anything that seems out of the ordinary to him. I really think his vision is significantly impaired as he barks at and tries to attack the garden gnomes and statues in planters along our route. He even tries to go after dogs INSIDE their homes if he can hear them barking. Leo, on the other hand, will approach every living creature we run across, ready to make friends and love on them. We have several "community cats" that we see on our rounds who look at him askance, turn tail, and strut off when he tries to make friends. When Turk growls and lunges at him, Leo takes

13

it as an invitation to play and is ready to wrestle. He doesn't growl or bark back. In fact, I can't say that I have ever heard him growl in any situation. Jake and Charlie found this all too athletic and required too much effort, so they just stood back and observed.

Once we are back home from our walk and breakfast is over, we work on whatever chores must be taken care of that day. Leo's "help" is often less than beneficial. He needs to supervise the trash collection to ensure I don't throw away anything he deems worth keeping. One of his favorite activities is to see how many pieces he can shred a tissue into and how far he can distribute said pieces before I put an end to the activity. Changing the sheets includes several minutes of hide-and-seek in the covers. Sweeping or mopping is considered a "keep away" game.

All the toys that I collect from the floor before I can run the vacuum are suddenly irresistible and must be removed from the box again to be enjoyed and artfully scattered around the living room. Laundry is an acceptable solo activity as long as he gets to sit on the steps outside the back door to be sure I don't go farther than the shed where the washer and dryer are located. Folding clothes, however, he considers a team sport.

There is one tendency that really bothers me with Leo's behavior (other than the constant licking). It is rather annoying since, knowing how intelligent he is, I am sure he knows what he is doing is unacceptable. As I said before, we are out, nearly every morning, for at least 30 minutes but, some days, we will no sooner get back to the house than he promptly goes into the hall bathroom, where I have an emergency potty pad on the floor, and he poops not on that pad, but on the bathroom rug! It is NOT ok. I am very thankful that said poop is firm and easy to pick up with a paper towel but come on! We were just outside! He had plenty of time to go! He routinely gets praise and treats for doing his business outside! I get the feeling sometimes he is telling me that while I may be in charge of most aspects of his life, HE has control over those events.

We visited with Aunt Ruth two or three times a day. She was skeptical about him at first. She grew up on a farm where ALL animals were kept outside. No dogs or cats in the house for ANY reason. Animals slept in the barn. It didn't take long for him to win her over, especially after her health became bad enough that we had to stay with her, and we had to curtail most outings to protect her from COVID. He would sit at her feet while she sat in her recliner reading or watching TV. He would just stare at her until she relented and reached down to scratch his head. He never tried to jump up on her, but everyone else sitting in a recliner (or rocking chair) was fair game. She greeted him with, "Well, hello little man. What are you up to today?" each time we came in. He was skittish around her cane and walker until he got used to them, but he was always gentle and friendly toward her. It wasn't long before I noticed her "saving a bite for Leo" when she had a treat. She was always amazed that when I placed his leash on the floor (a retractable contraption) and went about gathering her trash, putting groceries away or doing other chores, he would lay down and not move until I came back and picked it up. Any other time he was right on my heels. I called it his anchor, and it was something he learned on his own, I didn't intentionally try to teach him to do it, but it certainly comes in handy. I didn't have to worry about Aunt Ruth or myself tripping over him.

Leo misses her now that she is gone. He still wants to turn up her driveway when we walk up her street.

7

Caring for Leo

One of the perks of getting your dog from the "Get Your Pet" site is a free checkup with a local veterinarian. His appointment went very well; he had perfect weight and was in excellent health. I had copies of his records, so I knew his next shots were due in November. We did have to make arrangements for getting him neutered. I'm not sure why his former owners hadn't done it because I am sure it was recommended, but that oversight was taken care of when we got back from our Ohio trip.

Next on the list of tasks was grooming. Leo has a Bichon-type coat, thank goodness (I would hate to have to keep the long, flowing Shih Tzu-length hair brushed out). He doesn't shed, even when brushed—another plus. Grooming is the most significant expense of taking care of him. He needs a haircut every six weeks max. If we wait any longer, the hair on his face curls into his eyes and his ears become matted. It also gets long between his toes and soaks up water like a sponge. His ears, tail, and "mustache" pick up what I call "velcro seeds" when he noses around in the grass. When he is trimmed short, there is less hair to catch them, but I still have to spend part of the evening searching for strays that like to attach to his face. I have tried trimming this area myself, but that doesn't go over well at all.

Leo is generally quiet. I did not hear him bark at all for more than two months, until nearly Thanksgiving, when the cousins came down from Georgia to visit Aunt Ruth. They have a dog named Biscuit, a Shih

Tzu/something else mix, similar in size and appearance to Leo stockier. Biscuit is a barker.......an unrelenting barker. They got along and played well together, but as soon as Leo's attention focused elsewhere, Biscuit would bark incessantly to reclaim his attention. Leo seemed mystified by all that noise at first, but THEN he found his voice! It was a very loud visit from that point on. Even Aunt Ruth, deaf as she was, would tell them to be quiet. Leo still doesn't bark a lot, but, stubborn fella that he is, he will bark at me: 1. When he wants to go out, and I am occupied with something else. 2. When he thinks he has been ignored long enough and wants to play. 3. If I haven't watched the time closely enough and it is past the time we usually go out to pick up the mail, after a potty stop, between 4 and 5 pm. He will absolutely let me know I am falling down on the job. 4. Occasionally, if I am engrossed in my writing or studying, I don't head for bed when he thinks it is time. He usually sits and stares at me until I give up and head for the bedroom.

8

Traveling with Leo

Leo loves to ride in the car, whether it is a quick trip to the mailboxes or several hours on the road. He patiently waits for me to run into the store or the post office. Since it is summer in Florida there aren't too many days he can go out with me.

We made a trip to Ohio, by car, in November while the cousins were here to watch over Aunt Ruth. He rode in his car seat, moved up to the passenger seat from the back.

He is a very pleasant traveling companion. No demands or complaints. He only had one episode of anxiety when, due to a detour off the main highway in a wet, dismal twilight, when I couldn't find a safe place to pull over, and he was becoming desperate for a pit stop.

We arrived in Ohio to snow. He was fascinated by that cold, white stuff and plowed his nose along the ground, trying to figure out what that cold stuff was. I had a coat and a sweater for him, thinking a Florida dog might suffer in Ohio's November weather. Nope. It didn't bother him a bit. Of course, I had put off his routine haircut until we got back, so he had some extra insulation.

He overwhelmed our 15-year-old (45-pound) Lab-mix dog at our Ohio home. Leo wanted to make friends and play, but Harlee wasn't interested in wrestling, racing around the living room, or chasing a thrown toy. Harlee looked askance at him when overtures were made but then plodded off to find a quiet place to nap. Leo decided playing fetch with my husband was an acceptable substitute activity.

Harlee

9

Pros and cons: Puppy vs. Adult Dog

Now that I have shown you what life with Leo is like, I will summarize some important factors to consider when trying to decide on a puppy vs an adult or, maybe, a juvenile dog.

Puppies are messy. Granted, some adult dogs can be too, but puppies will be worse. A puppy will need training, a LOT of training; from how to walk on a leash to teething/chewing issues to potty training (almost as challenging as trying to train a toddler, and certainly not something you would want to try to take on at the same time).

Juvenile dogs are still mentally puppies in many respects, but, the size of an adult dog (yes, canine teenagers) and they can be just as challenging. They are often still in that chewing stage where nothing they can reach is safe. They learn quickly how to get into closets, drawers, and hampers. There is nothing more embarrassing than to have your dog drag a pair of underwear into the living room when you have guests. You will want many chew sticks and toys specially made for aggressive chewers.

An adult dog will bring along a certain amount of baggage coming into your home. (I will use "he" though most scenarios could also apply to females) Is he psychologically scarred because he lost his family and he feels abandoned? Was he abused? Is he food aggressive (a definite drawback if you have young children running around)? Does he have an absolute loathing of men wearing boots or women in high heels? (We had a dog once when my husband was still in the Marine Corp, who had obviously been kicked by a man dressed in utilities with combat boots. She was very friendly toward him when he was in civilian clothes, but when she saw him in uniform, she would cower and hide.) An adult dog, like an adult human, has a past that might have left scars.

10

The Benefit of a Family Dog

I think all children should grow up with a dog. It teaches them empathy and responsibility. It makes them aware of the needs of other creatures, but young children and small puppies can be an unfortunate mix. Neither has a sense of limits or the ability to understand the actions of the other. I have seen young children grab a puppy or kitten around the neck and try to carry it around or try to stuff it in a box (or the toilet). While learning to walk, an unsteady toddler could fall on a small puppy, such as a chihuahua, which could be fatal for the pup.

The young puppy won't understand that your two-year-old's skin, without a layer of fur, is much more fragile than the siblings he is used to wrestling with, and it will bite and scratch while playing. This could possibly leave teeth marks or scratches, maybe even injuring a child's eye.

Both toddlers and puppies end up with EVERYTHING in their mouths. That cute little puppy probably has worms and will be chewing on your baby's fingers and toys. Almost all puppies need to be wormed once they start to eat solid food.

An adult dog will come to you with a certain amount of baggage. It is important to consider the members of your family when making your decision about the animal you want to bring home. Do you have young children? A small, anxious dog might not be right for you. A chihuahua whose previous home was with a quiet, sedentary 80-year-old probably wouldn't be suitable in a home with young children.

Do you have rambunctious teenagers who like to roughhouse? The noise and physical grappling might trigger a dog who has been physically abused.

Has the animal been spayed/neutered? That would be something to look into as soon as possible.

You might also consider adopting a senior dog. Many end up homeless through no fault of their own. Unfortunately, some people surrender their elderly dogs to replace them with a younger ones. You could give them a secure, happy home in their final years. There are benefits, too. They don't have the same attention or exercise needs as younger animals. A leisurely stroll once or twice a day is usually sufficient. This might be the way to go if yours is a more sedentary lifestyle.

Any breed of dog that was raised with love and patience can be a wonderful pet, but some breeds have a reputation for aggression. The breeds that have historically been used as guard dogs are products of selective breeding over the centuries. They were carefully chosen and bred for the desired traits to be enhanced in their offspring. They may interpret rolling around on the floor and pulling at each other (as boys, and some girls, tend to do) as an assault and leap in to protect their family members. In recent years, these dogs have been irresponsibly bred for even greater aggression and viciousness by unsavory dog fight promoters. These dogs would be best left to the experienced owner who understands how to set and enforce expectations of obedient behaviors. They do not belong in the typical family home. They need to be seen by the dog as the Alpha of their pack and are not safe with an untrained.

11

Where to look

Adopting an adult dog as a rescue/re-home, rather than buying a puppy at a pet store or breeder was a no-brainer for me. Aside from the fact that I didn't want to train a puppy again, the prices asked for them are obscene, even for mutts. I just looked online at a couple of litters of Yorkie puppies, 10 and 12 weeks old. The prices were $2000-5000! Even some rescue sites wanted $600-900 or more for pure breeds! Now, I had no problem paying for vet care or shots needed but that was still way out of line with my thinking. I paid a nominal fee for Leo but got several perks, too.

When looking for a new pet, you need to evaluate your circumstances carefully. When you decide what you really want and what makes sense for your family, you can start checking Humane Societies, shelters, pounds, or even veterinarian offices. In my small town and others, in Ohio, there are many locations with bulletin boards offering pets; supermarkets, beauty shops and other businesses, branch libraries, and recreational facilities. You don't see that as much in big cities but Small Town America still has that more personal touch. Pet stores and breeders would be last on my list.

Since newspapers are slowly going the way of the dinosaurs, they are seldom a useful option, but If your community has a newsletter, you might find listings there.

12

Keywords to Search

As I said before, I had a wider selection to look at with online sites. If you start your search by using your location in a search request with keywords such as "animal shelters" or "Humane Societies near me," you'll have a list of places to start. A lot of times, you can indicate the distance you are prepared to travel. You can also search "Humane Society in (nearby cities/counties)", "No-kill shelters" or "Border Collie (or any breed) Rescue". Your local dog pound might yield results and chances are, those animals will be in more dire straights, facing euthanasia if not adopted promptly. My veterinarian, in Ohio, has a bulletin board in his waiting room where people can post animals they are looking for or want to re-home.

Please, though, I urge you to stay away from pet stores and puppy mills. Those cute, darling puppies likely come from parents living in deplorable conditions (unless, of course, they are breeding show dogs). In many cases, the dogs are kept in cages to be bred repeatedly until they are too old or sick to be of any further use. The only way the practice can be stopped is by removing the market.

13

Making your choice

Once you make the decision that you DO want a pet, and you start looking online, you will find yourself becoming anxious, like waiting for the lottery numbers to be announced. When you see the picture of a dog that melts your heart, you will need to fill out the form, and the waiting game begins. Many rescues don't have regular hours or staff. That means you might not get a response for days.

If you are offered the chance to meet that dog, you should try to get as much information as possible before you make an appointment to meet. You might discover in further discussion that the dog you have already claimed in your heart is totally unsuitable for your family or won't fit into your lifestyle. Make sure to keep a level head with common sense engaged.

I know some people have adopted animals from across the country, deciding with only pictures and conversation as a guide to spend hundreds of dollars to have the dog shipped to them. That seems to me like a dangerous way to go. You might find, when the dog gets to you, that you have another Cujo on your hands, or he might just dislike you on sight. You may find you are now the owner of a sickly animal with a seizure disorder or heartworms. Most rescue sites are probably ethical and honest in their dealings, but there are probably nearly as many that aren't. A face-to-face meeting with the dog and the owner/caregiver will give you a much better idea of the temperament, health, and socialization of that particular animal and if you can form a successful bond.

14

Online Sources

To get you started, here are some of the online sites I checked. I finally found Leo on "Get Your Pet." Each site has different requirements. All of them have pictures. There are some excellent articles available to guide you on breed traits and temperaments, expected life span, known health problems in each breed, and training tips.

https://getyourpet.com/

https://www.adoptapet.com/

https://www.petfinder.com/

I also ran across some pet re-homing sites on Facebook. My sister, a long-time Yorkie rescuer, sent me links to a couple of pages that I watched for a while, but none of the dogs I was interested in were close to me. I wasn't going to drive several states away to look at a dog I might not even bring back with me. I checked Pekingese sites (we had Pekes when I was growing up) and Papillon rescue pages. (Those are small breeds that I know enough about that I might want one.) There are multiple pages for almost any breed of dog.

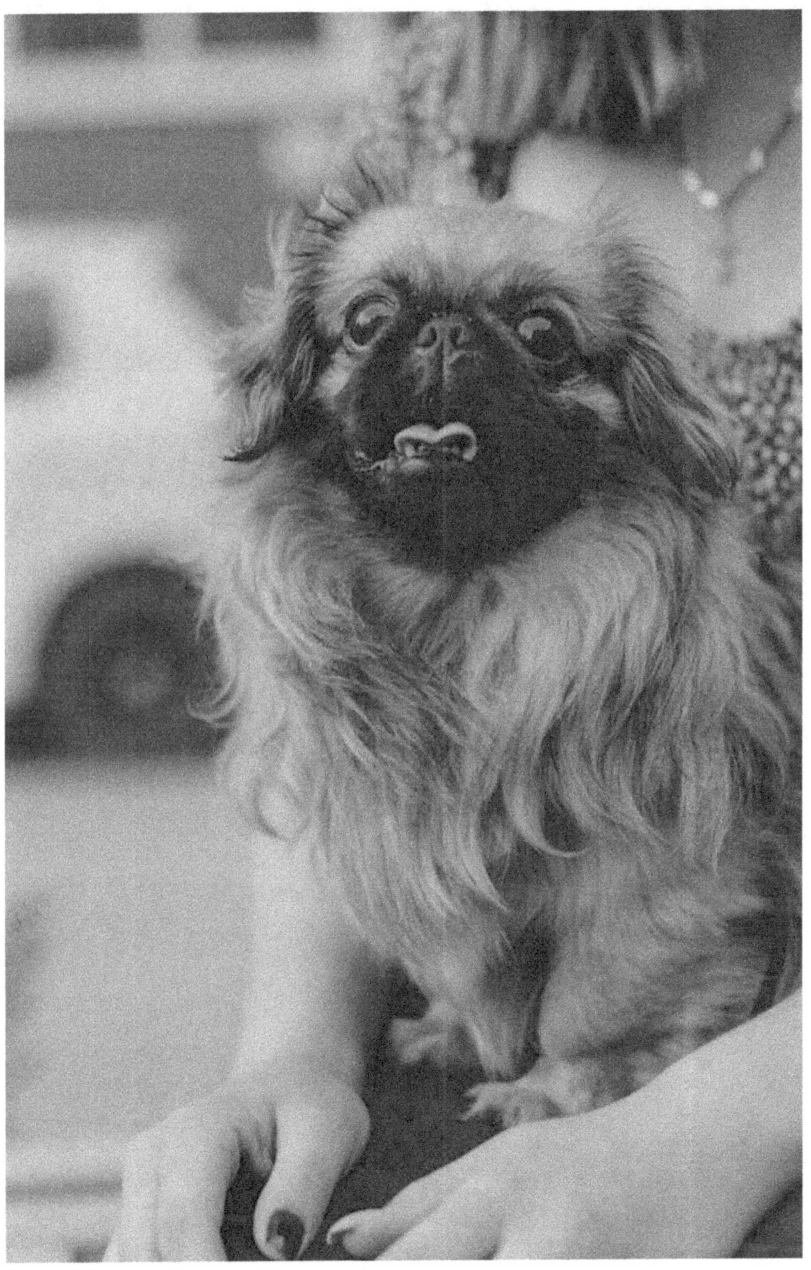

When doing searches online, some rescues were location-specific, and others had ways to search in multiple states/cities. A few pages I ran across: Pets for Re-homing. Pets to a Good Home. Adopt-a-Pet. I think I put "Re-home Pets" in the search bar at the top. I was very leery of one page that said the pets were free. While I'm all for finding all animals a new home at a reasonable price, that "Free" didn't sit well with me. I envisioned dogs being snapped up to use as bait dogs. I guess I have become too cynical as I've gotten older.

When it comes down to it, your decision about whether you get a puppy or rescue an older dog will be your personal choice. BUT, you could be lucky enough to be offered a puppy from the litter of an OOPS event in the life of your friend's dog. You may have a neighbor or family member who can no longer care for their pet through no fault of their own. If you find yourself in these circumstances, you might acquire a loyal companion without suffering the angst of trying to make those hard decisions. In fact, sometimes those are the very best ways to get your pet. If possible, and you don't already know the dog, meet and develop a friendship, or at least an acquaintance with the animal to lessen the shock of the change in their reality.

15

Conclusion

Whatever path you take to find your ideal companion, I hope your journey turns out to be as rewarding as mine has been with Leo. He is now firmly entrenched as a member of our family.

If you enjoyed Leo's story or found this information helpful in your search for your new pet, I would appreciate it if you would leave a favorable review for the book on Amazon.